Civil War
Heroines

by Joan Nichols

Editorial Offices: Glenview, Illinois • Parsippany, New Jersey • New York, New York

Sales Offices: Needham, Massachusetts • Duluth, Georgia • Glenview, Illinois
Coppell, Texas • Ontario, California • Mesa, Arizona

Even as a child, Sarah Grimke hated slavery.
She said slavery "marred [spoiled] my comfort
from the time I can remember myself."

The Abolitionists

Some women were heroines before the Civil War began.
These women were abolitionists. They wrote books and
pamphlets against slavery. They spoke out against it in public
lectures.

Sarah and Angelina Grimke were two early abolitionists who
came from a family of wealthy slave owners in South Carolina.
However, they believed all people were created equal.

The Grimke sisters moved to the North, where they spoke out against slavery. Many people criticized them, believing that women should not give public lectures. Other people praised them, because these former slave owners who spoke out so strongly against slavery impressed them.

Sojourner Truth, born an enslaved person, knew the horrors of slavery from her own life. Her height, sharp wit, and strong voice made her a powerful speaker at anti-slavery meetings.

Angelina Grimke was Sarah's younger sister. In school one day, she fainted when she saw an African American boy who had been badly beaten.

Two Harriets

Harriet Beecher Stowe was not a Southerner or a former slave. She was born in Connecticut, which was a **free state** in 1811. In 1832 she moved to Ohio, which was also a free state at that time. Kentucky, a **slave state**, was across the Ohio River. This was the first time that Stowe came in contact with slavery and escaping enslaved people.

She heard about an African American woman who carried her baby across the icebound Ohio River. Stowe used this story when she wrote *Uncle Tom's Cabin*. Her book appealed to readers' emotions. It made them see that enslaved people were fellow human beings. The novel became a bestseller all over the world.

Most abolitionists spoke publicly and wrote books to fight slavery. Harriet Tubman risked her own life and freedom by helping enslaved people escape. She traveled south eighteen times, leading people north, where they would be free. She was never caught, even though there was a large reward offered for her capture.

When President Abraham Lincoln met Harriet Beecher Stowe, he supposedly said, "So you're the little woman who wrote the book that started this Great War!"

Harriet Tubman, born an enslaved person, escaped in 1849. She was so thrilled to reach free territory that she said, "I looked at my hands to see if I were the same person."

The Woman Behind the Song

You may have heard the song that begins, "Mine eyes have seen the glory." Julia Ward Howe had heard some Union soldiers singing a popular marching song called "John Brown's Body," about John Brown, a famous abolitionist. She was asked to write different words for that song. The next day she wrote new words for the tune and submitted them to *The Atlantic Monthly* magazine. Soon "The Battle Hymn of the Republic" was sung all over the North.

The Home Front

After the South **seceded**, the fighting began. On the **home front**, away from the main battles, women fought their own war. Many women worked hard and showed courage defending their homes and supporting the cause in which they believed.

Almost half the men in the North joined the army or were called up by the **draft**. So did about 80 percent of the men in the South. These men left family farms and businesses for women to run. And the women did, even when the war seemed far away. There were shortages of food and clothing, especially in the South.

Poor women had to go to work to support their families. They did this by sewing uniforms and making rifle cartridges.

Women still found time to help the soldiers by joining together to roll bandages, knit socks, and sew clothing for them. Women also sent the soldiers packages of blankets, sheets, towels, and food.

Nurses

More than two thousand women volunteered as nurses during the Civil War. Most nursed their own husbands, brothers, and other relatives.

For instance, Ellon McCormick Looby learned that her husband Rody had been wounded. In 1864 she and her four-year-old son John traveled from New York to Virginia to nurse him. She continued working as a nurse in the same hospital until the war ended.

Clara Barton

Clara Barton felt sorry for the Union soldiers because they were not getting all the supplies they needed. The wounded soldiers needed better medical care. On her own she sent out a call for food and medical supplies. Friends helped her deliver them to battlefields in Virginia and Maryland. She also helped find soldiers who were missing and helped their families get in touch with them. With this experience she later founded the American Red Cross. Today this organization does the same kind of work that Clara Barton did during the Civil War.

Sally Louisa Tompkins

Sally Louisa Tompkins opened a hospital in a friend's house in Richmond, Virginia. To run it, she used money she inherited. Her hospital did such a good job healing the wounded soldiers, she was given the rank of cavalry captain. From then on she was called "Captain Sally."

Nurses and officers pose together in front of a house that served as part of a military camp.

A Writer and Nurse

Have you read the book *Little Women?* The events in it take place during the Civil War. In the book the mother of the March family goes to a military hospital to nurse her wounded husband. Louisa May Alcott, who was also a Civil War nurse, wrote *Little Women*. In 1862 she went to Washington, D.C., to help care for the wounded.

Louisa May Alcott

A month later she got sick and had to return home. She wrote about her experiences in a book called *Hospital Sketches*.

Susie King Taylor

Laundress, Teacher, Nurse

Even though Susie King Taylor was born enslaved, she learned how to read and write. When she was fourteen, she was freed by Union troops before slavery was abolished. She married Sergeant Edward King, a member of the 33rd United States Colored Troops, a **regiment** of former slaves.

She lived with the regiment, which was a common thing for women to do in those days. She did the soldiers' laundry and taught them how to read and write. When members of the regiment were wounded in a raid, she nursed them. She continued working as a nurse for the next four years.

Woman Doctor in the War

Dr. Mary Edwards Walker wanted to be a doctor in the Union army, but very few women were doctors at that time. At first the army refused to make her a medical officer. So she volunteered to work without pay. When she did this, she became the army's first woman surgeon. Later she was appointed a medical officer. In 1864 she was captured by the

Mary Edwards Walker

Confederates and spent four months in prison. After the war, she was awarded the Congressional Medal of Honor. This is the country's highest military honor, and she was the first woman to ever receive it.

Spies

Some women became spies for the North or the South. They learned important military secrets from the enemy and told these secrets to military leaders on their own side. Some women were **couriers** and carried messages across enemy lines.

Rose O'Neal Greenhow

Because Rose O'Neal Greenhow had many important friends in Washington, D.C., she was able to get information from them secretly. Then she told the Confederate army what important information she learned. The Confederate government sent her on a mission to Europe as a courier. She drowned on the return journey because her boat capsized. The weight of the gold coins she was carrying to the South dragged her down.

Rose O'Neal Greenhow

Elizabeth Van Lew

Elizabeth Van Lew

Elizabeth Van Lew was a Southerner who was also a secret abolitionist. She pretended to bring food, medicine, and books to Union prisoners in Richmond, Virginia. She told the Confederate guards she was just being kind. Actually, the prisoners gave her important information, sometimes using a code she invented.

Soldiers

At least four hundred women disguised themselves as men and joined the armies of the North and the South. Some women joined to be with their husbands or brothers. Many served because they believed their side's cause was just. Others went simply for the adventure and excitement. A few even worked as spies, and almost all of them served bravely on the battlefield. Most of these women soldiers were found out only when they became ill or wounded. Nurses often discovered these women among their patients.

Canadian Sarah Emma Edmonds served in the Union army as "Franklin Thompson."

Loreta Velazquez was known as Confederate officer "Lt. Harry T. Buford." She wore a false beard and mustache as part of her disguise.

Teachers

When Union soldiers entered the South, enslaved people flocked to them in search of freedom. But the enslaved people also needed food, shelter, work, and medical care. Most of all they wanted education, because most of them had been forbidden to read and write. Now they wanted to learn. Concerned Northern men and women came south to help them, and many of the women became teachers.

This engraving shows the Freedmen's School in Vicksburg, Mississippi.

Charlotte Forten

Charlotte Forten was the first African American schoolteacher from the North to go to the South to teach former slaves. She had a good education, and she saw the need to help others. She taught on St. Helena Island, South Carolina, and kept a diary of her experience.

Glossary

courier a messenger

draft a law that requires men of a certain age to serve in the military, if called

free state a state where slavery was not allowed

home front the area or activities near home for a country at war

regiment an army group with a large number of soldiers

secede to break away from a group, as the Southern states broke away from the United States

slave state a state where slavery was allowed